NINEVEH AND THE
OLD TESTAMENT

NINEVEH
AND THE
OLD TESTAMENT

ANDRÉ PARROT

Curator-in-Chief of the French National Museums,
Professor at the Ecole du Louvre, Paris,
Director of the Mari Archaeological Expedition

PHILOSOPHICAL LIBRARY
NEW YORK

Translated by B. E. Hooke
from the French
NINIVE ET L'ANCIEN TESTAMENT
(Delachaux et Niestlé, Neuchâtel
Second edition 1955)

Published 1955, by the Philosophical Library, Inc.,
15 East 40th Street, New York, 16, N.Y.

Printed in Great Britain for Philosophical Library, Inc., by
The Camelot Press Ltd., London and Southampton

CONTENTS

MAR 7 1957

LIST OF ILLUSTRATIONS

FOREWORD

IN APRIL 1950 we arrived at Mosul. During the twenty years spent in Iraq or in Syria, we had never had an opportunity to cross the 'Assyrian triangle'. Once again we realized how necessary it is to see in order to understand, and especially to hold in the memory. Knowledge gained from books is certainly not enough, for names which are not attached to any reality are nothing more than ghosts. Ghosts of cities, shadows of men, vague floating shapes, without solidity, though one tries to capture it with the aid of a drawing, a photograph or a vivid description. All students of archaeology know this by experience: nothing can replace actual contact with the object. That is why museums are so important; because there one can recognize the long chain of human history stretching out continuously from its beginning, but in which, instinctively we have a special interest in detecting and observing the first links. But the object is a prisoner in its glass case. Torn from its natural surroundings it has lost its true speech. Nevertheless it exerts a pull, it beckons one to take the road. It is impossible to contemplate the Assyrian reliefs in the Louvre or the British Museum without calling up the image of Nineveh.

[9]

But to visit Nineveh is to run the risk of a bitter disappointment, if one expects to see murals or palaces. The murals have either been destroyed or have crumbled away, although a few faint lines still remain. As for the palaces, they are completely obliterated and from their foundations have risen the two mounds which now stand in the Tigris plain. On one of them a village and a minaret bear witness to the life which still goes on above a tomb. On the other there is nothing but a little grass and some small strips of cultivated land where once were royal residences, the temples of Nabu and Ishtar. That day a few hens came out of a hovel of stone and rubble and went pecking here and there. It was not easy to remind oneself that one was treading the soil where warriors and despots had trod and where once the palaces of Sennacherib and Ashurbanipal had stood. But after all, is it not better that nothing remains, and that from the hill of Quyundjiq only the horizon is to be seen? The snow-covered mountains of Kurdistan, the green fields and the silver thread of the Tigris? Waters at least remain unchanged.

Nineveh, Nimrud, Khorsabad, Asshur—in four days we had visited them all. Four 'Assyrian days', too short for all there was to see, but filled to the brim because they were so short, and because a prearranged programme prevented their being extended. However, thanks to our cordial reception by the Dominican Fathers, and their thorough knowledge of the country, everything was so well organized that not an hour was lost or wasted. It is easy to understand, therefore, that ever since then our memory of Nineveh is bound up with that of Mosul and the white cell in the monastery where, every evening of that short stay, we were able to meditate, only a few yards from the Assyrian capital, on the vanity of empires and the fate which awaits all of them.

Translator's note. Throughout this volume biblical quotations are not taken from any of the recognized English versions of the Bible, but are translated from the French.

I

The Exploration of Nineveh

NINEVEH IS EXPLICITLY mentioned in three books of the Old Testament. First of all in Genesis, where its foundation is attributed to Nimrod. From the land of Shinar (Babylon), 'cradle of his empire', that 'great hunter before Yahweh' went up to Assyria[1] where he built 'Nineveh, Rehoboth-ir, Kalakh and Resin, between Nineveh and Kalakh' (10.11-12).

This very important notice is followed by a marginal note, which most certainly refers to Nineveh: 'That is the great city' (v. 12b). The second mention is found in the book of Nahum, where the prophet foretells the destruction of the 'bloody city' (3.1) or pronounces a 'Te Deum celebrated shortly after that event and attributing that signal deliverance to Yahweh'.[2] We shall return later to this remarkable passage. Finally, everyone knows how, because he would not obey the command of Yahweh

[1] Father de Vaux translates otherwise: 'From that country went out Ashur, who built Nineveh . . .' *La Genèse*, p. 69.

[2] *Bible du Centenaire*, note to Nahum, 1.1.

[13]

who had sent him to Nineveh, Jonah took ship at Joppa, and what afterwards befell him there. However, the son of Amittai finally executed the order given to him, and went to Nineveh, 'a city divinely great' (Jonah 3.3), so great that to cross it was 'three days' journey'.

It is grievous to think that Nineveh shared the fate of many other great metropolitan cities of the ancient east: destruction and dereliction. But Lucian of Samosata was exaggerating when he put into the mouth of Mercury, when Charon was carrying him away, those decisive words: 'Nineveh is so completely destroyed that it is no longer possible to say where it stood. Not a single trace of it remains.' No one will dispute the savagery of the destruction, but traces of the city are still, and always have been, visible. The huge mounds of rubbish which, even today, stand facing Mosul and on the other side of the Tigris, are eloquent witnesses. It has been necessary to explore and examine them—a long and arduous task which, even after a century of labour, cannot be said to be finally and completely accomplished. Like Babylon, Nineveh has not yielded up all its secrets.

The exploration of Nineveh has been going on for a hundred years,[1] but before the arrival of excavators, the feet of many travellers had trodden the historic site. On the left bank of the river, the two

[1] R. C. Thompson, *A Century of Exploration at Nineveh*.

tells of Quyundjiq and Nebi Yunys—the latter with a mosque and the 'tomb of Jonah' (Pls. 1 and 2, p. 32)—corresponded to what was known about the site of the city, although it was not possible to be precise about its size. Jonah's 'three days' journey' stimulated the imagination and, for a long time, complicated research. In the seventeenth century, John Cartwright, who had 'carefully examined' the ruins, estimated that the perimeter of the city wall measured fifty-eight miles and that three chariots abreast could easily have been driven on it. Do not let us criticize too severely this imaginative valuation, which has been corrected by more sober judgements, such as K. Niebuhr and, in particular, C. J. Rich, to whom we owe not merely a description but also a plan of the ruins (November 1820); let us pass on to Botta, with whom archaeological investigation began.[1]

P. E. Botta, who had been appointed French Consul at Mosul, took up his position in 1842, being then forty years old. He already knew something of the

[1] In my *Archéologie mésopotamienne*, I, will be found a summary of researches, in chronological order and under the names of the excavators who carried them out: Botta, Layard, Place, Rassam, Smith (pp. 37-104); King, Campbell Thompson (pp. 163-66); Campbell Thompson, Hutchinson, Hamilton, Mallowan (pp. 412-19). Among English publications, besides the reports of excavators, two books which provide a wealth of information may be mentioned: C. J. Gadd, *The Assyrian Sculptures*, 1934, and *The Stones of Assyria*, 1936.

East but he had never been to Mesopotamia. This was the fulfilment of his youthful dreams, since he had long felt the call of archaeological excavation. There were ruins only a few yards distant from his house. In 1842 with a few workmen he made a start at excavating the *tell* of Quyundjiq. If not a total

I. Assyrian reliefs from the palace of Sargon II at Khorsabad

failure, it was only partially successful, and to any-one who knows the place, this is by no means surprising. Botta was beginning to be distressed about these 'almost fruitless' researches, when, in March 1843, the natives showed him another *tell* which might prove to be more profitable. This mound, called Khorsabad, was about ten miles away and some 'figures and inscriptions' could be seen there at earth level. The consul, who at first was sceptical, sent a servant there who confirmed the rumour. Botta went there straight away, and immediately finds appeared: walls of impressive construction and, at the foot of the walls, sculptured reliefs (fig. I). In April 1843, Botta announced his discovery, being

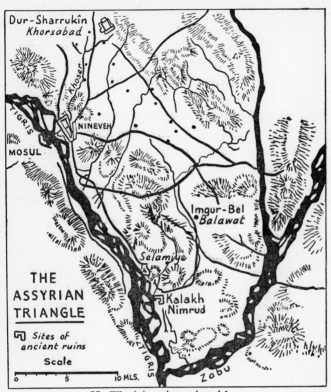

II. The 'Assyrian triangle'

convinced that he had found, at Khorsabad, the
city of Nineveh.[1]

Work at Khorsabad went on till October 1844. In

[1] This explains the title of the official publication, *Monument
de Ninive découvert et décrit par M. P.-E. Botta, mesuré et dessiné par
M. E. Flandin*, 5 vols. in folio, Paris, 1849-50.

B   [17]

February 1847, a convoy arrived at Paris with a sensational load: the first Assyrian reliefs, huge sculptured slabs revealing a hitherto unknown civilization and originating—as inscriptions were to prove quite clearly—not in Nineveh but in another Assyrian capital, Dur-Sharrukin, a kind of ancient Versailles, built entirely by Sargon II (721–705 B.C.) and abandoned shortly after his death.

Botta had returned to France. The events of 1848 were fatal to his career, for he was a staunch royalist, and he was given the least honourable posts in the service—Jerusalem, and then Tripoli in Barbary.[1] He was lost to archaeology, but not before he had inspired others who immediately went into action. In 1845 the Englishman Layard arrived in Mosul, also in quest of Nineveh. He first directed his efforts to a *tell* farther south called Nimrud (fig. II) where another capital city of the Assyrian kingdom was to be revealed, Kalakh. However, he devoted a few months to Quyundjiq, which was again identified with Nineveh, and which became the scene of fierce competition between France and England.

In January 1852 Victor Place came to Mosul as

[1] I take this opportunity to correct an error in *Archéologie mésopotamienne*, I, p. 45, where I wrote 'Tripoli de *Syrie*'. This information, which I took from Gadd, *Stones of Assyria*, p. 22, was incorrect, as I was informed by the French Consul-General at Jerusalem, René Neuville. Cf. my 'Centenaire de la fondation du musée assyrien au musée du Louvre', in *Syria*, XXV (1948), pp. 173-84.

French Consul. He decided to follow in the footsteps of his predecessor Botta and engage actively in archaeology. But in those days, when there were no regulations about antiquities, the rights of the first occupant of a site had the force of law. Place took over the earlier workings at Khorsabad without relinquishing Quyundjiq where Botta had been the first to start excavating (December 1842). But Layard had entered into Botta's labours and England had no intention of being dispossessed. Rawlinson, who was then British representative in Mesopotamia, signed an agreement with Place: Quyundjiq was to be divided: the northern part was to be excavated by the French, the southern by the English, in the person of a Chaldean Christian, H. Rassam. In defiance of the agreement, and anxious about the activities of unauthorized excavators, Rassam worked for several successive nights in the sector assigned to V. Place. In December 1853 his workmen, operating in a tunnel, uncovered the first reliefs in the series of Ashurbanipal's lion-hunt. Before Place knew of it, this valuable site was occupied, this time in daylight: France had decisively lost the site of Nineveh and with it two of the finest Assyrian palaces—those of Ashurbanipal and Sennacherib—with their fabulous wealth of reliefs and thousands of cuneiform tablets. From that time, England pursued the excavation of Quyundjiq with the utmost intensity. During the next few years a succession of excavators attacked the site: H. Rassam (1852–4), Boutcher, Loftus (1854–5); but the Crimean War and lack of funds thrust archaeology into the background. It was necessary also to study the documents which had been found and, in particular, the thousands of tablets from the library of Ashurbanipal where, later on, sensational discoveries caused considerable stir.[1] George Smith set out for Nineveh again, intent on epigraphy. A first expedition in 1873 was followed by a second in 1874 and by a third in 1876, in the course of which he died of sunstroke after a few days' illness, at the age of thirty-six.

The English were again obliged to have recourse to Rassam, whose aim was merely to scratch the surface of likely sites. For four years (1878–82) the work of pillage went on and Quyundjiq gave up its precious remains. In spite of all his contacts, Rassam did not succeed in exploring Nebi Yunus, where Hilmi Pasha, the Governor of Mosul, did some secret excavations, not without results. Protected by powerful taboos (a mosque, a cemetery, a village) the second mound of Nineveh remained inviolate.

However, the time had come for more scientific enterprises. The British Museum sent one of its young assistants, E. W. Budge, who, from 1888 to 1891, had to confine himself, for lack of means, to

[1] For further details, see *The Flood and Noah's Ark* (Studies in Biblical Archaeology No. 1), pp. 22 *et seq.*

clearing out the old diggings. The site was then closed again.

In 1903 L. W. King returned there, at first alone, later with R. Campbell Thompson. In 1905 professional assyriologists began to make attempts to introduce some order into the chaos by assigning to their architectural framework and archaeological background the objects and documents which until then had been excavated quite unsystematically. Then there was another long interval—twenty-two years—before the return of the archaeologists.

The veteran Campbell Thompson directed the expedition assisted by other technicians: first Hutchinson, later Hamilton and Mallowan. From 1927 to 1932 Quyundjiq was explored much more scientifically. Not only were the cleared areas more exhaustively examined, but stratigraphic excavations were made, with a view to reaching the earliest period of the city's existence, until virgin soil was found at a depth of some eighty-two feet below the surface. Starting from the Christian era the excavators penetrated, layer by layer, through the Assyrian periods to proto-historic times, in some places to about 5000 B.C. Thus, in 1932, the exploration of Nineveh, 'that . . . great city', was completed.

*   *   *

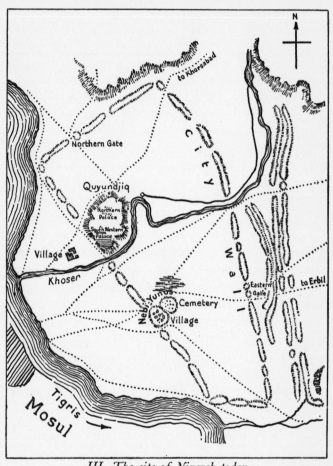

III. The site of Nineveh today

The Exploration of Nineveh

Nineveh (Assyrian: *Ni-nu-a*; Hebrew: *Nineveh*; Greek: *Ninos*)[1] stood on the left bank of the Tigris, possibly some little distance from the river.[2] Today two mounds cover the ruins of the ancient city; *Quyundjiq* to the north-west, *Nebi Yunus* (fig. III) to the south-east. Between them is a small river, the Khoser, which flows into the Tigris. Only Quyundjiq has been excavated. As already mentioned, Nebi Yunus,[3] with its burial ground, its mosque, the 'tomb of Jonah' and the village which clusters round it, could not be explored and probably never will be.[4] Quyundjiq measures, at its greatest area, about one mile in length and about six hundred and fifty yards in width. It stands about ninety feet above the plain, from which it rises almost sheer on all sides. It has

[1] The city is referred to in the Mari tablets as *Ni-nu-wa-a* (*ki*). It is written ideographically as ÈSH ḪA; see Pohl in *Orientalia* (1954), p. 256.

[2] Herodotus (1,193) has established that alteration of the river's course, which was very common in Mesopotamia. Thus Mari, which today is roughly one mile distant from the Euphrates, was certainly situated on the bank of the river about 3000 B.C.

[3] See traditions about Nebi Yunus collected by the Rev. Father Fieh in the *Bulletin du séminaire syro-chaldéen*, IV (1943), pp. 101-14.

[4] In the course of an excavation carried out in 1954 by the Director General of Antiquities of Iraq the remains of a palace of the time of Ashurbanipal (?) were discovered. Three statues of Pharaohs (Tirhakah?) were also unearthed, which must have been brought from Egypt as plunder by King Esarhaddon.

been estimated that this mound of rubbish represents 14,500,000 tons of earth, and that a thousand men, each shifting 120,000 tons a year, would take 124 years to remove the whole pile.[1] Nebi Yunus is only half as large, in area and cubic size (6,500,000 tons of earth). The buildings which cover it give it necessarily a different appearance, more mysterious but also more lively, that of daily life lived only a few feet away from the hidden remains of antiquity.

The stratigraphic excavation revealed that Nineveh was one of the oldest cities of Mesopotamia: sixty-four feet of debris represented its existence through ages going back to proto-historic[2] times, that is to say 5000 and 4000 B.C. The first *written* reference to the city is much later. It is to be found in a Cappadocian tablet discovered in Asia Minor on the site of Kultepe where there was a colony of Semitic merchants in frequent contact with Mesopotamia. Nineveh is mentioned in a cuneiform text (twenty-first century B.C.) inscribed on a clay tablet and the name is given in an ideogram: a fish drawn in the middle of a city, an obvious

[1] These figures given by Campbell Thompson are only approximate since an archaeological excavation is not a public undertaking, with a working day of fixed and regular length.

[2] R. C. Thompson and M. E. L. Mallowan, 'The British Excavations at Nineveh, 1931-1932', in *Annals of Archaeology and Anthropology*, XX (1933), pp. 71-186.

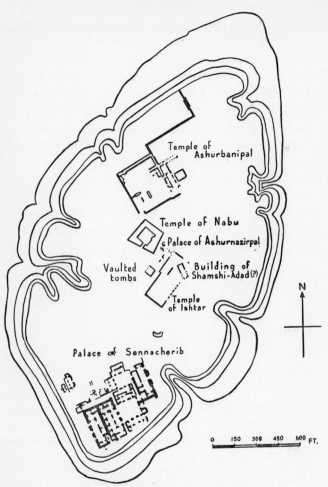

Temple of
Ashurbanipal

Temple of Nabu

Palace of Ashurnazirpal

Vaulted
tombs

Building of
Shamshi-Adad(?)

Temple
of Ishtar

N

Palace of Sennacherib

0   150   300   450   600
FT.

IV. The monuments of Nineveh

allusion to the goddess Nina whose emblem it was.[1]

A little later, Hammurabi (1792–1750 B.C.) in his Code describes himself thus: 'The King who in Nineveh, in *E-mish-mish*, glorified the name of the goddess Ishtar.' That Ishtar is pre-eminently the goddess of Nineveh is confirmed by an inscription of one of the ancient kings of Ashur, Shamshi-Adad (1823–1791 B.C.), which reads 'The temple *E-me-nu-è* in the land of *E-mash-mash*,[2] the old temple which Manishtusu, son of Sharrukin, king of Accad, built, fell into ruins'. Thus from the time of the kings of Accad (2500–2300 B.C.), Nineveh was dedicated to Ishtar[3] and there is no doubt that this goddess of love and war was specially venerated here in her character of warrior. The oldest temple of Nineveh seems therefore to have been that of the goddess of war. A most remarkable prefiguration of the fate of a people who engaged in unceasing warfare.

The second temple to be discovered, almost in the centre of the mound, was the shrine dedicated to Nabu, god of writing (fig. IV). No deity could have been more appropriate to this city, whose ruins were to yield tens of thousands of tablets.

[1] A connection will certainly be seen between Nineveh and Jonah, the man swallowed by a fish and the city containing a fish. . .

[2] Assyrian inscriptions always use the form *E-mash-mash*.

[3] E. Dhorme, 'Le plus ancien temple d'Istar à Ninive', in *Revue de l'Histoire des religions*, CX (1934), pp. 140-56. Reprinted in *Recueil Édouard Dhorme* (1951), pp. 585-99.

V. Slaves at work (relief from Nineveh) (from Layard, Monuments of Nineveh, II, p. 16)

Several palaces were also discovered: one, on the north, built by Ashurbanipal (662–628 B.C.), another, to the south, the residence of Sennacherib (704–681 B.C.). These were the most impressive, but architectural fragments attributed, among others, to Shalmaneser I (1273–1244), Tiglathpileser I (1114–1076), Adadnirari II (911–891), Ashurnazirpal (883–859), Tukulti-Ninurta II (890–884)

[27]

provide evidence of an extraordinary building activity on the part of the local rulers.

This is not the place to compile a list of the long series of dynasties which ruled the upper Tigris region for at least two thousand years.[1] The history of Assyria can now be written, thanks to the extensive documentation which has been exhumed during more than a hundred years. Nineveh is known to have held a position of the first rank among a number of famous cities. She rivalled in splendour the other royal cities of Ashur (*Qalaat Sherqat*) and Kalakh (*Nimrud*) and was in no danger of being eclipsed until Sargon II (721–705 B.C.) built a completely new capital less than thirteen miles away, Dur Sharrukin (*Khorsabad*). But at the king's premature death, his son Sennacherib (704–681 B.C.) restored Nineveh to its former state and made it in fact the capital of Assyria. Sennacherib had vast resources of wealth and man-power—from the Persian Gulf to the Mediterranean all the subject populations constituted an unlimited reserve of slave-labour (fig. V); he had a quarter of a century to restore, enlarge and beautify the city; temples, palaces, ramparts, streets, aqueducts, public gardens sprang up from the ground. This enormous building programme was completed and, without doubt, the

[1] Reference may be made to the author's *Archéologie mésopotamienne* II, where on pp. 348–59 is given the whole series of the Assyrian kings from its beginning in the tenth century B.C.

king would have made further additions if he had not been assassinated at Babylon.

His example was followed by his successors Esarhaddon (680–669) and Ashurbanipal (668–626). Assyria had never known a more brilliant epoch. Its palaces housed the hoarded wealth of the subject nations. Behind its double line of ramparts Nineveh seemed to be invulnerable. She continued to make the whole world tremble, but these warrior kings were also lovers of letters and the arts. Armies of sculptors decorated shrines and palaces with innumerable stone slabs carved with reliefs which celebrated the prowess of the king in hunting or in battle. Schools of scribes copied the literary works of the past, sacred and secular, and the library of Ashurbanipal boasted tens of thousands of books— that is to say texts, written in cuneiform on clay tablets which were then baked. We shall now consider that documentation, selecting from it characteristic extracts which will serve to confirm, amplify or illustrate passages in the Old Testament where Nineveh and Assyria confront Palestine and the kingdoms of Israel and Judah.

II

Epigraphic and Archaeological Sources

THE HISTORY OF the ancient east can be readily understood by looking at the map. Two great powers —Egypt and Mesopotamia—though thousands of miles apart, were to meet each other, with fateful consequences, on the field of battle. Between these colossi, a string of little kingdoms, 'buffer states', could not hope, either to preserve their independence or to remain unscathed, aloof from the conflict. Syria, Phoenicia and Palestine were directly in the line of march of the armies and their territories were continually trodden by the feet of invaders advancing from the Nile Valley or moving south from Anatolia or the banks of the Tigris. Leaving aside the events of the second millennium, when Israel had not yet appeared on the stage of history, we start with the beginning of the first millennium, at the point of time when Tiglathpileser I (1114–

1076) reached the Mediterranean. It was the time of the Judges in Israel (cf. the chronological table on p. 90), and though events were leading up to the institution of the monarchy, this was in order to oppose the Philistines rather than to guard against danger from the Assyrians, which was entirely unsuspected at that time and even up to the moment when the kings of Nineveh, Ashur or Kalakh made their appearance on the shores of Phoenicia. Tiglath-pileser I announced his victory thus: 'From my accession to the throne to the fifth year of my reign, my hand has conquered in all forty-two countries with their kings, from the banks of the lower Zab, the land of the distant mountains, to the banks of the Euphrates, the land of Hattu and the great sea where the sun sets.'[1]

Two hundred years later Ashurbanipal II (883–859) came and exacted tribute from the cities of Phoenicia; in his own words: 'The tribute due from the kings on the sea coast, that is to say, those of the land of Tyre, of Sidon, of the land of the Giblites . . . and of the city of Arvad in the midst of the sea, tribute of silver, gold, lead, bronze, vases of bronze, clothing of many colours, linen tunics, a large and a small monkey, ebony and box-wood, sharks' teeth,

[1] For all these comparisons we are indebted to Dhorme's authoritative study *Les pays bibliques et l'Assyrie*, Paris, 1911, in which are reprinted articles published earlier in the *Revue Biblique* (see Bibliography, p. 95).

produce of the sea, I received from them and they kissed my feet.'[1]

This geographical list runs from south to north. We recognize Tyre, Sidon, Gebal-Byblos (Ezek. 17.9), Arvad (Gen. 10.18; Ezek. 17.8). The king of Assyria could not advance any farther, either towards Damascus, where he would have met strong resistance, or towards Israel, where Omri or Ahab would certainly have offered opposition.[2] The end of the text exactly reports the facts, as a number of monuments proudly show and as we shall see on the obelisk of Shalmaneser in reference to Jehu.

* * *

Shalmaneser III (858–824) attempted what his father had not ventured to do. Not only did he extort further contributions from Phoenicia, but he set about attacking Syria and her allies—a federation of eleven kings, the three most important being: Adadidri of Damascus, with 1,200 war chariots, 1,200 horsemen, and 20,000 foot soldiers; Irhuleni of Hamath, with 700 chariots, 700 horsemen and 10,000 foot soldiers; Ahab (*A-ha-ab-bu*) of Israel

---

[1] Dhorme's translation in *RB*, (1910), pp. 60-1. The text is taken from the *Annals*, inscribed on stone slabs in the temple of Ninurta. This should be compared with the inscription on the magnificent stela discovered at Nimrud by Mallowan in 1951 and published by Wiseman, *Iraq*, XIV (1952), pp. 24-44.

[2] The *Annals* do not give the year of this campaign.

1. Nebi Yunus

2. Quyundjiq (André Parrot)

3. Obelisk of Shalmaneser III (British Museum)

(*Sir'-i-la-a-a*) with 2,000 chariots and 10,000 foot soldiers.[1]

These were by far the largest contingents and suggest that the military power of Israel was considerable and that her king had used all his efforts to furnish a body of shock troops. The cost of the war was a heavy burden to the northern kingdom, in view of the fact that all this material had to be imported: chariots from Egypt, horses from Cilicia, at a price of six hundred silver shekels for a chariot and one hundred and fifty silver shekels for a horse. This gives some idea of the wealth of a state which could spend so much of its resources on the equipment of its army.

The allies engaged Shalmaneser III in Upper Syria between Qarqar and Gilzau (854 B.C.). According to the Assyrian account, they were heavily defeated. In the words of the victorious king: 'With the supreme power with which the Lord Ashur endowed me, and with the strong weapons provided for me by Nergal who went before me, I fought against them. From the city of Qarqar as far as Gilzau I attacked them. I overthrew 14,000 warriors of their armies; like the god Hadad, I caused a deluge to overwhelm them; I piled up their corpses, I strewed the plain with their hosts. By my sword I made their blood flow in the hollows of the land. The plain was too small to hold their corpses, the earth was not able to bury them; I filled up the Orontes

[1] The so-called monolith inscription from Kurkh.

with their bodies. I captured in the battle their chariots, their horsemen, their horses and their armour.'[1]

It may be doubted whether the battle of Qarqar was as decisive as Shalmaneser III claimed. It is known that the war was not conclusive and that the Assyrian king returned to the attack several times. The kings of Syria, Irhuleni of Hamath, and Adadidri of Damascus (called Ben-Hadad in I Kings 20.1) continued to oppose him, but Ahab had withdrawn from the alliance, having little regard for the needs of his neighbours, especially the king of Damascus, his sworn enemy. It was, moreover, when fighting against him that Ahab met his death in his war-chariot (I Kings 22.34-38).

After Ahaziah and Joram, Jehu succeeded to the throne of Samaria. The menace of Assyria became more acute and, for the first time in the country's history, the king of Israel became a vassal and paid tribute. There is no mention of this in the Bible, but the fact is beyond dispute. On a fragment of the *Annals* of King Shalmaneser III, after a report of a victorious action against Hazael of Damascus (II Kings 8.28), the following words occur: 'Then I took

[1] Dhorme's translation in *RB* (1910), pp. 66-7. Text from the *Annals*. Ashur, Nergal and Hadad are three male deities in the Assyrian pantheon. In some of its details this account may be compared with the song of Deborah (Judg. 5). In both battles, rain played an important part, turning the land into a quagmire and impeding the movements of the chariots.

tribute from the Tyrians (fig. VI), the Sidonians and from Jehu (*Ia-u-a*), the descendant of Omri (*Hu-um-ri-i*).'

This notice is supported by the reliefs on the black

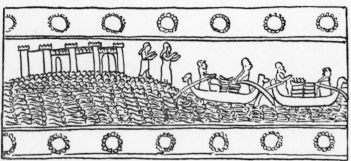

VI. Tribute brought to Shalmaneser III from Tyre (from King, Bronze Reliefs . . ., Pl. xiii)

obelisk, discovered at Kalakh and now in the British Museum. In the second section of this monument, (Pl. 3, p. 33) the king of Assyria is shown standing, while prostrated before him is a figure which must be Jehu, king of Israel. Six Assyrian officials are present, some forming the retinue of the king (one carrying the ceremonial umbrella) and some leading the procession of thirteen vassals bearing gifts (fig. VII). An inscription gives a short but explicit comment: 'The tribute of Jehu (*Ia-w-a*) son of Omri: I received from him silver, gold, a golden bowl, a golden vase with a pointed bottom, golden tumblers,

golden buckets, tin, a staff for a king and wooden
puruhtu.[1]

This monument is extremely important for biblical
archaeology. It is, moreover, the only example of a
secular monument on which is depicted a historical

VII. The Tribute of Jehu, king of Israel

personage from the Old Testament, whether Israelite
or Judaean.

In connection with Jehu it may be noted that the
reliefs dating from the time of Ashurbanipal II and
Shalmaneser III throw some light on the precise
meaning of a military term found in the book of
Kings. There is mention of a person who, according
to the Hebrew text, 'was the third on whose arm the
king leaned' (II Kings 7.2, 17), or again 'the third

[1] The obelisk of Shalmaneser III has been frequently
reproduced, and two photographs are given in this book. The
text is from J. B. Pritchard, *Ancient Near Eastern Texts*, p. 281.

[36]

VIII. The third man of the Assyrian chariot (from Layard, op. cit., *Pl. 42)*

who went with him' (II Kings 9.25). This 'third', rendered in the English Revised Version as 'captain', is really the person who is seen in the chariot, behind the king and the driver—in fact a third man (fig. VIII).[1]

*   *   *

[1] This has been pointed out by C. J. Gadd, *The Assyrian Sculptures*, p. 35. Father de Vaux, in *Les Livres des Rois*, renders it 'ecuyer' (groom). The *Bible du Centenaire* (note to II Kings 10.25) gives 'The man who rode in the third place in his chariot.'

Shalmaneser's grandson, Adadnirari III (805–782 B.C.) also laid a heavy hand on the west. The Assyrian armies drew nearer and nearer to Egypt, and thus to Israel, during the reign of Joash (II Kings 13.10). Once again the smaller kingdoms failed to realize that it would be to their advantage to form an alliance against the enemy, who continued to levy tribute. 'From the Euphrates to the great sea where the sun sets[1] I crushed under my feet the land of Hattu and the whole land of Amurru, the countries of Tyre, Sidon, Omri (*Hu-um-ri*), Edom and Philistia. I laid on them a heavy tribute.'[2] The Assyrians still called Israel by the name of the founder of the dynasty, Omri. Judah is not mentioned, an omission which is all the more curious in view of the fact that the three neighbouring countries, including Edom which is much farther south, are named. There is nothing in the Bible on this subject.

On the other hand, the Bible narratives are explicit about the much more important events which followed in the reign of Tiglathpileser III (745–727 B.C.). Neither Israel nor Judah emerged

[1] The Mediterranean.

[2] Dhorme's translation, in *RB* (1910), p. 185, of an inscription on a stone slab found at Kalakh. It was very probably Adadnirari III who took from Damascus to Hadatu (Arslan-Tash) the ivories which Thureau-Dangin discovered in 1928. These ivories are further discussed in the volume in this series which is concerned with Samaria.

unscathed from this new crisis, due to the rise to power of an ambitious monarch, who carried out his policy of expansion regardless of obstacles. His aims were achieved the more easily because Jeroboam II, one of the greatest kings of Israel, had died at Samaria (746 B.C.) and his legitimate successor, Zechariah, had been murdered by Shallum, who himself was executed by Menahem (II Kings 15.8-14). Menahem continued to pursue a policy of violence, which, however, did not save him from invasion. The official historian records it thus: 'In his time, Pul, the king of Assyria[1] invaded the land. Menahem gave him a thousand talents of silver in order that the king of Assyria might extend his hand to him and confirm him on the throne. And Menahem placed the burden of this payment on Israel; he exacted from all the great men, to pay the king of Assyria, fifty shekels of silver each.[2] So the king of Assyria turned back and occupied the land no more' (II Kings 15.19-20).

Thanks to the Assyrian documents, it may be estimated that this crushing tribute,[3] which Tiglathpileser

[1] Pul (Babylonian *Pulu*) was the name which the king of Assyria bore as king of Babylon.

[2] A text discovered at Nimrud in 1953 (*Iraq*, XV (1953), p. 135) shows that in the seventh century B.C. this was the usual price of a slave.

[3] One thousand talents=three million shekels. If the contribution was fifty shekels per head, there must have been sixty thousand 'great men' in Israel.

records, was collected in the year 738 B.C.; it is inadvisable, however, to insist on the exact date, for 'Menahem of Samaria' (*Me-ni-hi-im-me al Sa-me-ri-na-a-a*) was only one among a number of vassals—Resin of Damascus, Hiram of Tyre, Sibit-tibi'li of Byblos, etc.[1]

On this occasion, however, the kingdom of Judah did not escape, and the Hebrew and Assyrian documents agree. Ahaz was king in Jerusalem. Of him it was written: 'So Ahaz sent messengers to Tiglathpileser king of Assyria, saying, "I am thy servant and thy son; come up and save me out of the hands of the king of Syria[2] and the king of Israel,[3] who are risen up against me." And Ahaz took the silver and gold that was found in the house of Yahweh, and in the store-house of the king's palace, and sent it for a present to the king of Assyria.[4] And the king of Assyria hearkened unto him' (II Kings 16.17-8). '. . . King Ahaz went to Damascus for a meeting with Tiglathpileser, king of Assyria (fig. IX), and there he saw the altar which was at

[1] Text from the *Annals* written on stone slabs found at Kalakh.

[2] Resin (II Kings 16.5).

[3] Pekah (II Kings 16.5). It is this event to which the well-known intervention of Isaiah refers (Isa. 7.1-9). To him Resin and Pekah were only 'two tails of smoking firebrands' (v. 4).

[4] In similar circumstances, objects and precious metals were collected in the same way (I Kings 16.18-19; II Kings 12.18) as deliveries made to Ben-Hadad and Hazael of Damascus.

IX. *King Tiglathpileser III* (?) *besieging a city* (*from H. Gressmann*, Altorientalische Bilder. . ., *No. 125*)

Damascus[1] and king Ahaz sent to Urijah the priest the measurements and a model of the altar, giving the details of its structure. And Urijah the priest made an altar, exactly following the instructions that King Ahaz had sent from Damascus. He completed it before King Ahaz came back from Damascus' (II

[1] This was the altar of the god Hadad of Damascus; today a mosque of the Ummayyads stands on the site of his temple, where, in 1947, a relief decorated with a sphinx was found (see *Syria*, XXVI (1949), pp. 191-5).

Kings 16.10-11). In the Assyrian sources there is again only a very brief mention. Among the vassals, after the king of Ashkelon and before the king of Moab, occurs *Ia-u-ha-zi* (Ahaz), *Ia-u-da-a-a* (Judah).[1]

It is interesting to note that Tiglathpileser, in answer to the appeal of his vassal Ahaz, inflicted severe punishment on Israel and Damascus, initiating the system of deportations, which the Assyrians carried to extreme lengths.[2] As additional security, he placed on the throne of Samaria a certain Hoshea, whom he had assisted in his conspiracy against Pekah (II Kings 15.30).

The Assyrian account of these events is extant. 'The house of *Hu-um-ri-a* (Omri, i.e. Israel) . . . all his people, and their goods, I sent away to Assyria. They overthrew their king *Pa-qa-ha* (Pekah) and I made *A-u-si* (Hoshea) king over them. I received from them ten talents of gold, a thousand (?)

[1] A tablet found at Kalakh. A tablet discovered at Nimrud in 1950 gives some very interesting information about Tiglathpileser's campaign against Philistia (734 B.C.). Hanunu, the king of Gaza, abandoned, in his flight, a whole collection of treasures (statues, steles) and . . . his wife. Thus Tiglathpileser was able to recover a number of statues of Assyrian gods as well as one of himself, made of gold. See Wiseman, 'Two historical inscriptions from Nimrud' in *Iraq*, XIII (1951), pp. 21-2; A. Alt, *Kleine Schriften* . . ., pp. 150-62.

[2] II Kings 15.29. All the towns mentioned belonged to the kingdom of Israel which had begun to be dismembered before it was completely devastated.

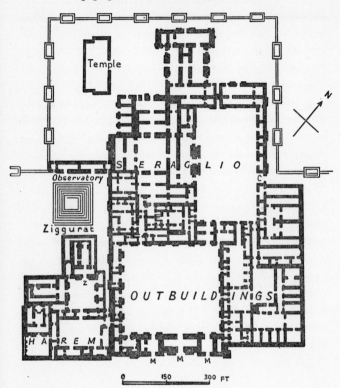

X. Plan of the palace of Sargon II at Khorsabad (from Thomas' reconstruction)

talents of silver as tribute and I carried them away to Assyria.'[1]

But things were to become still worse for Israel.

[1] Pritchard, *ANET*, p. 284. Text of *Annals* found at Kalakh.

[43]

Tiglathpileser was succeeded by his son Shalmaneser
V (727–722) and Hoshea seized the opportunity to
try and free himself from the yoke of Assyria,
encouraged in this attempt by the fact that the
Phoenicians were also in revolt. There was an
immediate reprisal, of which no mention is made in
the Assyrian documents but which is briefly recorded
in the book of Kings: 'Shalmaneser, king of Assyria,
came up against Hoshea, who became his servant
and paid him tribute' (II Kings 17.3). The passage
continues: 'But the king of Assyria discovered that
Hoshea was conspiring against him; he had sent
representatives to So,[1] king of Egypt, and did not
pay the tribute to the king of Assyria as he had done
year by year. So the king of Assyria shut him up in
prison and put him in chains. Then the king of
Assyria invaded all the land and marched on
Samaria and besieged it for three years. In the ninth
year of Hoshea, the king of Assyria conquered
Samaria and carried Israel away to Assyria' (II
Kings 17.4-6).[2]

*　　　　*　　　　*

The biblical tradition, which seems to attribute

[1] Another version gives *Seve*, to be identified with the Egyptian general *Sib'e*.

[2] This version, from the Israelite point of view, corresponds
with the Judaean account in II Kings 18.9-11.

the taking of Samaria to Shalmaneser,[1] differs from
the Assyrian documents which are quite explicit on
this point and give the credit to Sargon II (721–705)
who had become king at the death of his brother.[2]
The siege, which Shalmaneser began in 724 B.C.,
lasted for three years. This says much for the
resistance offered by the city and for the means and
the resources which enabled it to sustain for so long
an attack conducted by troops hardened to such
warfare and better equipped. But the disproportion
between the adversaries was too great and Samaria
fell. Sargon II (Pl. 3, p. 00) commemorated his
victory in a number of inscriptions found in the vast
palace which he spent six years building at Dur-
Sharrukin, not far from Nineveh.

A stone slab of a doorway proclaims proudly:
'Sargon, conqueror of Samaria (*Sa-mir-i-na*) and of
all Israel (*bît-Hu-um-ri-a*).' The so-called Display text
is more explicit: 'I besieged and conquered *Sa-me-
ri-na* (Samaria). I took away captive 27,290[3] of her

[1] Father Pohl maintains (*Orientalia* (1954), p. 266) that
Shalmaneser was the conqueror of Samaria, which seems
impossible. See the last text found at Nimrud and published
by C. J. Gadd in *Iraq*, XVI (1954), p. 180.

[2] For a long time Sargon was regarded as a usurper. A text
of Asshur, deciphered in 1933, has established this relation-
ship: Sargon and Shalmaneser were brothers, sons of Tiglathpileser.

[3] The Prism of Sargon, discovered at Nimrud in 1952, gives
27,280 prisoners and 200 chariots, *Iraq*, XVI (1954), p. 180.

inhabitants, I seized fifty chariots which I found there. The rest (of the inhabitants) I allowed to remain. I placed my general over them and imposed on them the same tribute as the previous king.'[1]

This put an end for ever to the kingdom of Israel. Her capital had been captured and the inhabitants—or at least the nobles and the upper classes—had been taken into captivity: 'He settled them in Kalakh and on the banks of the Habor,[2] on the river of Gozan and in the cities of the Medes' (II Kings 17.6). This first deportation was followed by another, in a different direction. The evacuated population (fig. XI) was replaced by peoples brought from other subjugated territories: 'The king of Assyria brought men from Babylon and from Cuthah and Avva and from Hamath and from Sepharvaim and settled them in the towns of Samaria in place of the children of Israel' (II Kings 17.24). Evidence of this resettlement is to be found in an Assyrian document, in a passage in the *Annals* of Sargon: 'I rebuilt the town (Samaria) better than it was before and settled therein people from countries which I myself had conquered.'[3]

[1] Dhorme's translation in *RB* (1910), pp. 372-3. An inscription from Khorsabad.

[2] A tributary of the Euphrates, on the left bank. This is in upper Mesopotamia.

[3] Text in Pritchard, *ANET*, p. 284. The cities mentioned are widely scattered; it was a hotchpotch of peoples coming from Syria and Arabia as well as Babylon. The towns mentioned in the book of Kings may be identified as follows: *Cuthah* is today

XI. Deported populations going into exile (relief of Ashurbanipal at Nineveh, from monuments in the Louvre)

In the life of the Assyrian king, the capture of Samaria was only one episode among many others, for Sargon spent more time on the battlefield than in the splendid residence he had built with the labour of thousands of slaves, and with the blessing of the great gods Ashur, Nabu, and Marduk. He was

the mound of Ibrahim, between Baghdad and Babylon, the city of the god Nergal; *Avva* has not been located; *Hamath* is Syrian Hama, on the bank of the Orontes, noted for its gardens and its waterwheels; *Sepharvaim* is no doubt identical with *Sibraim* (Ezek. 47.16) between Hama and Damascus.

[47]

constantly on the move, for ever exposing conspiracies, crushing insurrections. Several times he had to send his troops to the west, for an alliance had been formed, initiated by the king of Ashdod and supported by Egypt, for the purpose of breaking the Assyrian tyranny.

The prophet Isaiah opposed this rash policy and exerted all his influence to dissuade Hezekiah, the king of Judah, from taking any part in it. But the king was in a state of uncertainty and was without doubt subjected to considerable pressure. The king of Babylon, Merodach-Baladan,[1] the enemy of Sargon of Assyria,[2] attempted to draw him into the alliance and this was the real reason for his sending an embassy to Jerusalem (II Kings 20.12–14). But Isaiah denounced the illusory hope that with the help of Egypt it would be possible to overcome Assyria (Isa. 20), whose *tartan*[3] (commander-in-chief) had even then besieged and taken Ashdod (Isa. 20.1). Once again all the kinglets had to submit and pay tribute. The land of Judah (*Ia-u-di*) is

[1] This is Marduk-apal-iddin II, who withstood Sargon for ten years. It is at this point that the official visit of the Babylonian delegates took place and not at the time of Sennacherib, for during his reign Marduk-apal-iddin could not have been in Babylon for more than nine months (703 B.C.).

[2] He caused a cylinder, which Marduk-apal-iddin had placed in Uruk, to be taken back to Kalakh (Nimrud). See *Iraq*, XV (1953), pp. 128-9.

[3] In Assyrian, *turtânu*: commander-in-chief.

4. Sargon II, conqueror of Samaria (relief in Turin Museum, from Weidner in *Arch. f. Orientalforsch.* XI, p. 133)

mentioned along with Philistia, Edom and Moab, and its offerings were laid at the feet of the god Ashur. Its independence was no doubt preserved, but at what a cost and for how long?

Such was the general situation at the time. The Assyrians were invincible; from Elam to the island of Cyprus, the whole of Eastern Asia lay under their sway. Their troops were stationed on the frontiers of Egypt.[1] In their huge palaces on the banks of the Tigris was gathered the wealth of the whole world, and thousands of slaves cringed beneath their whips. At that moment came news of the tyrant's death. He had been killed during an expedition to the land of Tabal in north Elam and his body had not been brought back to the capital for the appropriate funerary honours. This event must have been greeted everywhere as the herald of a fateful change. It is possible that an echo of it has been preserved in that remarkable dirge[2] in the book of Isaiah,[3]

[1] A. Alt. *Kleine Schriften* . . ., II, pp. 226-41 (see Bibliography, p. 95, below).

[2] This and the following translations are taken from the *Bible du Centenaire*. Not all scholars recognize Sargon in the person to whom the prophet refers. The names of Sennacherib, Ashur-uballit and Nabonidus have been suggested. It should be remembered that Sargon was king of Babylon from 709 B.C. after his victory over Marduk-apal-iddin.

[3] Quite recently S. N. Kramer, in *Biblical Parallels from Sumerian Literature*, October 1954, p. 14, offered as a parallel to this chapter of Isaiah a cuneiform tablet which describes the arrival of the Sumerian king Ur-Nammu in the underworld.

D

←—

5. Sennacherib at the siege of Lachish (British Museum)

who, as already mentioned, was a contemporary of Sargon.

'How has the oppressor been brought to his end,
How are his cruel deeds concluded?

Yahweh has broken the rod of the wicked,
The sceptre of tyrants,

He who savagely smote the people,
Smiting them without respite,

He who, in his wrath, subdued the nations,
Subdued them without mercy.

Now all the earth knows rest and quietness;
She breaks forth into cries of joy.

Even the cypresses rejoice at thy downfall,
(As do) the cedars of Lebanon:

"Now that thou art fallen, none arises
against us to cut us down."[1]

Sheol[2] beneath is aroused
To welcome you when you come.

[1] The kings of Assyria got their supplies of timber, which was scarce in their own country, from the forests of Amanus and Lebanon. Other references to this practice may be found in II Kings 19.23; Isa. 37.24. These levies are depicted on the famous reliefs of Khorsabad which adorned the eighth court of the palace; they are now in the Louvre (Gallery XXI of Oriental Antiquities). The two small islands shown have recently been identified with Tyre and Arvad. The incidents shown must therefore have taken place in Phoenicia.

[2] The dwelling-place of the dead, here personified.

All the kings of the nations
  Rise up from their thrones,

All together they speak
  And say to thee:

"Behold, thou also hast become weak like us,
  Thou art even as we are!

Is this he who made the earth shake,
  Who overturned kingdoms?

Who laid waste the world
  And destroyed cities,

Who never let his captives go free to return
  to their land?

All the kings of the nations,
All are at rest with honour,
  Each in his place,

But thou, thou liest far from thy grave,[1]
  Like an untimely birth, a thing of horror." '
                     (Isa. 14.4-10, 16-19)

*   *   *

At the death of Sargon his son Sennacherib succeeded him (705–681). Though the succession

---

[1] This detail exactly applies to Sargon of whom it is said, in a cuneiform text, that 'he was not buried in his house' (Cf. Dhorme in *RB* (1910), p. 389, note 4).

took place without any internal upheavals,[1] it was marked by a general rising of the oppressed nations, whether in Babylon or in Philistia. It is not surprising to find Judah involved in these affairs.[2] Hezekiah was on the throne and the kinglets of the seaboard dragged him into the rebellion. It was harshly suppressed. In 701 B.C. the king of Nineveh came with troops and a battle was fought in the Philistian plain at Elteqeh. The allies were wiped out and Hezekiah, who had captured a certain *Padi*, an adherent of Sennacherib, hastened to release his prisoner. But the king of Judah did not extricate himself so easily. The biblical tradition and the Assyrian account agree on this point and it is interesting to compare them.

TAYLOR PRISM	II KINGS 18.13-16
Since *Ha-za-qi-ia-u* (Hezekiah) did not submit to my yoke, I besieged forty-six of his strongholds, fortified places, and innumerable small villages at their gates. I took them by means of ramps, battering rams, together with assaults by foot-soldiers using mines	13. Now in the fourteenth year of Hezekiah, Sennacherib, king of Assyria, attacked all the strongholds of Judah and took them.

[1] Mallowan's recent excavations have in fact revealed, in the palaces of Nimrud, traces of a revolt and of pillage following the death of Sargon. It is necessary, therefore, to correct this statement. *Dies diem docet* . . .

[2] Biblical sources: II Kings 18–19; II Chron. 32; Isa. 36–37; II Chron. 32. 1–23.

TAYLOR PRISM   II KINGS 18.13-16

and saps. I captured and re-
moved 200,150 persons, young
and old, men and women,
horses, mules, asses, camels,
large and small stock without
number and I took them as
plunder. The king himself
(Hezekiah) I shut up in Jerusalem, his royal city, like a bird
in a cage. I built towers against
him, and anyone who came
out of the main gate of the
town, I chastised. The towns
which I raided I cut off from his
country and gave them to *Mi-
ti-in-ti,* king of Ashdod and
Padi-i, king of Acheron and
Is-mi-en, king of Gaza. I
diminished his country but I
increased the tribute and the
gifts due to me as his overlord.
These I required of him over
and above the tribute paid
every year. Hezekiah, overcome by the glory and the
terror of my sovereignty, and
because his picked troops and
the irregular forces which he
had concentrated at Jerusalem
to defend it, had deserted, sent
to me, afterwards, at Nineveh
my imperial city: 30 talents of
gold, 800 talents of silver, precious stones, antimony, *daq-
gas-si* stone, large slabs of por-
phyry, beds inlaid with ivory,

14. Then Hezekiah, king of
Judah, sent messengers to the
king of Assyria at Lachish,
bidding them say to him: 'I
have sinned; cease from
attacking me. Everything you
put on me I will submit to it.'
The king of Assyria caused
Hezekiah, king of Judah, to
pay 300 talents of silver and
30 talents of gold.
15. Hezekiah gave him all
the silver that was found in

TAYLOR PRISM	II KINGS 18.13-16
ceremonial thrones of ivory, elephant hides, ebony-wood and boxwood, coloured garments, dyed tunics—violet and crimson—objects of copper, iron, bronze, and lead, chariots, bucklers, lances, body armour, daggers, belts, bows and arrows, innumerable weapons of war, as well as his daughters, concubines, musicians both male and female. He sent his envoys to bear the tribute and to do obeisance.	the house of Yahweh and in the store-house of the king's palace. 16. At that time Hezekiah stripped [of their plating] the doors of the sanctuary of Yahweh, as well as the pillars which . . . the king of Judah had covered [with metal] and he sent it all to the king of Assyria.

These two accounts agree in essentials; the difference in the amounts (eight hundred talents of silver in one and three hundred in the other) may be due either to the exaggeration of the conqueror or to the fact that the value of the Babylonian talent was three-eighths of that of the Hebrew talent.[1]

In any case the sum demanded was crushing. That Hezekiah had to perform an act of submission is confirmed by other shorter notices. On a bull from Nineveh is the following inscription: 'I laid waste the large district of Judah (*Ia-ú-di*) and made the overbearing and proud Hezekiah (*Ha-za-qi-a-a*), its king, bow in submission.'[2] A text from Nebi Yunus

[1] This explanation is given in the *Bible du Centenaire*, see note *g* to II Kings, 18.14. The same view is expressed by A. Pohl, *Historia populi Israël*, p. 130.

[2] *ANET*, p. 288.

records likewise: 'I laid waste the large district of Judah and put the straps of my (yoke) upon Hezekiah, its king.'[1] There is therefore no problem in connection with this phase of the history.

But it is quite otherwise with regard to the rest of the biblical account (II Kings 18.17-19.37), which has no parallels in the cuneiform documents and has caused scholars much perplexity. Is it an account of the same incident with different details,[2] or does it refer to an episode in another of Sennacherib's campaigns,[3] in the course of which he laid siege to Jerusalem?

In the writer's opinion one single campaign of 701 B.C. is in question, and the account in Kings[4]

[1] *ANET*, p. 288.

[2] The view supported by Adolphe Lods in the *Bible du Centenaire*, note *c* to II Kings 18.13, and by Father de Vaux, *Les Livres des Rois*, p. 195 note *a*; by H. Haag in *RB* (1951), p. 350 and other exegetes such as Kittel, Alt, Rudolf, M. Noth.

[3] The opinion of Dhorme in *RB* (1910), p. 512, who adduces very powerful arguments, among others, that king Tirhakah, Pharaoh of the twenty-fifth dynasty, mentioned in II Kings 19, was not reigning in 701, but only from 690 onwards. It may be pointed out, however, that before his accession he occupied a very important position in the Egyptian army. This is also the interpretation offered by A. Lods and by Canon G. Riccioti, *Histoire d'Israël*, I, p. 489. On the other hand, W. F. Albright (*BASOR*, 130 (April 1953), p. 8 *et seq.*), still maintains that there were two campaigns, arguing that Tirhakah was only nine years old in 701 and could not have engaged in any military action against the Assyrians earlier than 688.

[4] II Kings 18.13-19.37. Cf. N. H. Snaith's study, *Notes on the Hebrew Text of I Kings 17-19 and 21-22*, 1954; A. Alt, *Kleine Schriften . . .*, II, pp. 242-9 (see Bibliography).

gives an elaborated version of events connected with the siege of Jerusalem, which, be it noted, is implicit in the short phrase of the Taylor Prism which refers to Hezekiah shut up in 'his royal city like a bird in a cage'; and this is confirmed by the statement in II Kings that the people of Jerusalem were reduced to the last extremity of need (II Kings 18.27)!

In the author's view, the course of events may be reconstructed as follows, by making use both of the biblical account and the Assyrian documents. At the outset it is suggested that the very bare account in II Kings 18.13-16, does not describe the beginning of Sennacherib's campaign but summarizes the *whole* campaign. It is a *résumé*, a framework, into which the accounts which follow and which describe a series of episodes, are to be inserted.

Sennacherib has arrived on the Philistian plain and attacks the border towns of Judah (II Kings 18.13). He makes a stand before Lachish, and begins to besiege it. Hezekiah immediately takes steps to defend his capital (II Chron. 32.1-8), at the same time sending envoys to the Assyrian king at Lachish (II Kings 18.14).

Sennacherib is in fact concentrating his efforts on the siege he is conducting[1] and which is to end in a victory for him (fig. XII). In the meantime, while

[1] This siege, though not mentioned in the Assyrian *Annals*, is depicted on a well-known relief found at Nineveh in room XXXVI of the palace of Sennacherib. We shall return to this later.

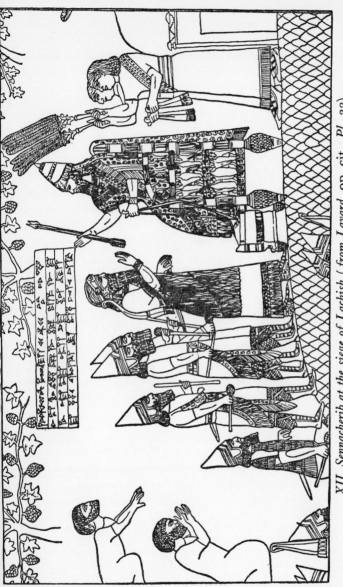

XII. Sennacherib at the siege of Lachish (*from Layard, op. cit., Pl. 23*)

he is still engaged on these operations, he sends a detachment of troops to Jerusalem as escort for three high officials who are instructed to conduct negotiations: The tartan (*tartânu*=general, commander-in-chief), the rab-sâris (*rab-sharish*=chief eunuch) and the rab-shâqé (*rab-shâqé*=chief cup-bearer). Biblical tradition, as recorded here (II Kings 18.17), has exactly reproduced the Assyrian titles.[1] Of the three personages mentioned, only the cup-bearer plays an active part.

The scene is a most remarkable one. At the foot of the city wall, in the valley of Kedron, a parley takes place between the two groups of envoys: the Assyrians on the one hand, the men of Judah on the other. The names of the latter are given: Eliakim, Shebna[2] and Joah, also high officials as befits plenipotentiaries: a steward of the palace, a scribe and a chancellor. The conversation is in Hebrew, but Hezekiah's envoys ask that Aramaic should be used, a language which they understand but which will not be intelligible to the soldiers on the wall who are listening. . . . The Assyrians refuse their request, and address themselves to the besieged population, for whose benefit the cup-bearer draws an idyllic

[1] Early translations have, mistakenly, taken these titles to be proper names; thus Segond, the synodal version, etc.

[2] The tomb of Shebna has been discovered at Shiloh, see N. Avigad, in *The Israel Exploration Journal*, vol. 3 (1953), pp. 137-52, and the author's article in *Semeur Vaudois*, 12th June 1954.

picture of the pleasures of life in exile (II Kings 18.31-32)!

The Jerusalemites report the conversation to their king who informs the prophet Isaiah. The prophet is entirely unmoved by this attempt at bluff and announces that, on the contrary, the king of Assyria will be forced to beat a retreat and will return to his own country where he will meet a violent death (II Kings 19.5-7).

The Assyrian envoys therefore depart with a negative answer. They did not, however, rejoin Sennacherib at Lachish but at Libnah (II Kings 19.8-9). Lachish in fact had been captured, as is shown on the relief from Nineveh.[1] The inscription runs: 'Sennacherib, king of the world, king of Assyria, seated on his throne of state, inspects the plunder from *La-ki-su* (Lachish) (Pl. 5, p. 49 and fig. XII).' The king is indeed preparing to receive his conquered enemies. They are all on their knees begging for mercy. At a short distance may be seen an incident in the siege: the city is being attacked with artillery but is being vigorously defended. From a tower, the garrison is shooting arrows and flinging stones and even torches. But from one gate fugitives or prisoners are emerging, with bundles on their

[1] See also Diringer, 'Sennacherib's Attack on Lachish', in *Vetus Testamentum*, I (1951), pp. 134-6. The results of the excavation of Lachish have recently been published by O. Tufnell, *Lachish*, III, 1953.

shoulders. Farther away, and as if to demonstrate to the defenders the fate which awaits them, Assyrian soldiers are impaling three naked men (fig. XIII).

At Libnah Sennacherib receives news of the arrival of the supporting troops from Egypt, led by 'Tirhakah, king of Ethiopia' (II Kings 19.9). It is *at this point* that the battle of Elteqeh should be placed.[1] The Egyptian army is driven back. Sennacherib takes advantage of its retreat to exert pressure again on Hezekiah and sends a second embassy (II Kings 19.9*b*).[2] The conditions are harsh in the extreme,[3] and Hezekiah's cry of despair may be readily understood (II Kings 19.15-19). He had to obey, however, and hand over tribute amounting to 30 talents of gold and 300 talents of silver (II Kings 18.14*b*), besides all those objects enumerated in the Assyrian texts. However, an unexpected event forced Sennacherib to leave Palestine in haste. The book of Kings records it thus: 'That same night the Angel of Yahweh came out and smote 185,000 men in the Assyrian camp. The next morning, on awakening, only dead bodies were to be seen everywhere.

---

[1] It is quite clear that the Assyrian account does not preserve the chronological order of events. H. Haag rightly emphasizes this point (*RB* (1951), p. 354).

[2] Here we part company with a number of exegetes who regard II Kings 19.9*b*-35 as a *parallel* account of the incident which has already been described in II Kings 18.17-19.9*a*.

[3] Father Pohl takes a less serious view of the situation, see *Orientalia* (1954), p. 266.

XIII. Siege of Lachish (*from Layard*, op. cit., *Pl. 21*)

Sennacherib, king of Assyria, struck camp and departed. He went back and dwelt at Nineveh' (II Kings 19.35-36).

There is no mention in any Assyrian source of this dramatic incident and precipitate departure. The annalists of Nineveh were subject to a censorship and the official records did not tell everything. But Herodotus (II, 141) refers to an Egyptian tradition according to which the army of 'Sanacharibos, king of the Arabs and the Assyrians', was halted on its march to Egypt by swarms of rats which gnawed every bit of rope or leather in its equipment. Since they could not use their armour, the troops had to go in flight. It is well known that rats are carriers of epidemic diseases, especially plague,[1] and it might well be that both the biblical narrative and the passage in Herodotus refer to this.[2] Thus Sennacherib was forced to retire and returned to Nineveh.

[1] The allegorical romance of Albert Camus, *La Peste*, gives a modern picture of the propagation of that scourge, which Jean La Fontaine calls 'that terrifying evil'.

[2] Dhorme, who supports the theory of a second campaign of Sennacherib in Palestine, after an expedition to Arabia (which would be vouched for by a fragment of an inscription reported by Scheil), considers that 'the privations endured by the army on its way through Arabia, the unwholesome water supplies available', were all 'factors which encouraged contagion' (*RB* (1910), p. 518). This retreat, occasioned by an epidemic, is not universally recognized. H. Haag disputes this interpretation and believes that Sennacherib evacuated Palestine in consequence of the severe losses he suffered in fighting against the Egyptians (*RB* (1951), p. 358).

Isaiah's prediction (II Kings 19.7*b*) was to be fulfilled twenty years later.[1] The king was in fact assassinated. The Bible records it explicitly: 'One day, when he was prostrating himself in the temple of Nisroch,[2] his god, his sons[3] Adrammelech and Sharezer slew him with the sword. They fled to the land of Ararat. And Esarhaddon, son of Sennacherib, became king in his place' (II Kings 19.37; Isa. 37.37).

There is confirmation of this event in a cuneiform document. Ashurbanipal, grandson of Sennacherib, states, on the one hand, that the assassination took place in a temple, and, on the other hand, that it was at Babylon. He also records that when he captured Babylon (in 648 B.C.) he slew 'as a funerary sacrifice' those of the murderers who were still alive and on the very spot, 'between the *shêdu* and the *lamassu*',[4] where the crime had been committed.

*   *   *

[1] The Bible narrative compresses into two verses (II Kings 19.36-37) events (return to Nineveh, assassination) which were separated by twenty years (700-681).

[2] No doubt this is Marduk. See Dhorme, *RB* (1910), p. 519, where it is shown how the word 'Marduk' might become 'Nisroch'.

[3] Dhorme, *op. cit.*, p. 520, suggests that the assassins were a son of Sennacherib, Arad-Belit or Arad-Malkat (cf. *Adrammelech*) and one of the officers whose name denoted the year 682-681, Nabu-shar-usur (cf. *Sharezer*).

[4] These are statues of gods or tutelary spirits. It is not known exactly who they were, because no bulls or winged lions, like those of the Assyrian temples or palaces, have been found in Babylon.

Esarhaddon, whose authority must have been shaken by the murder of his father, was a man of ferocious energy, able to turn to advantage the most unfavourable circumstances. In less than two months he had re-established his position and in February or March 680 he ascended the throne which he occupied till 669 B.C.

Esarhaddon need not be further discussed except for his contact with Judah, where Manasseh was then king (II Kings 21.1). His reign was a long one (687-642 B.C.)[1] and in the course of it he continually made advances and concessions to the ruler of the day, whose dealings with his vassals were no light matter. Of Sidon, for example, he records: 'Abdimilkutte its king who fled before my attack into the sea . . . I caught like a fish . . . and cut off his head.'[2]

It is probably Abdimilkutte, in company with Tirhakah, 'king of Ethiopia', who is depicted on the steles found at Sendjirli[3] or Tell Ahmar, kneeling before the king who arrogantly holds them on a leash, with a ring through their lips (fig. XIV). Amos is certainly alluding to this barbarous treatment when he says to the great ladies of Samaria: 'The days are coming when

[1] The chronology adopted here is that of Father de Vaux, *Les Livres des Rois*, p. 208, note *b*.

[2] Text from Prism B, in *ANET*, p. 291; extract in Dhorme, *RB* (1911), p. 203.

[3] According to H. Brunner, *Arch. für Orient. forsch.*, XVI, 2 (1953), p. 258, it would more probably be Ushanahurn, son of Tirhakah.

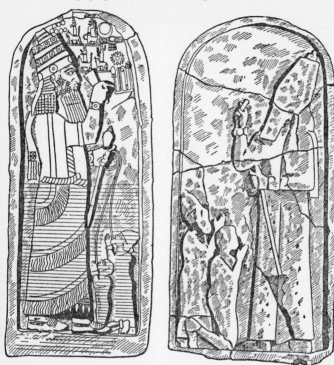

XIV. *Esarhaddon holding Abdimilkutte, king of Sidon, and
Tirhakah, king of Ethiopia on a leash*

they shall lead you away with hooks and those who
still survive with fish-hooks' (4.2).[1] Decapitations

[1] A passage in II Kings 19.28 also refers to this: 'Because
you have raged against me and your arrogance has come up
into my ears, *I will put a ring in your nostrils and a bridle on your lips.*'
The passage is repeated in Isa. 37.29. See also Ezek. 29.4;
38.4.

were also quite a common practice of those times. They are illustrated in a number of Assyrian reliefs (fig. XV) and provide a vivid commentary to the account in II Kings 10.6-8, in which Jehu, claimant to the throne of Israel, is described as using these savage methods.[1] It can readily be understood that in the face of such a demonstration, possible opponents would hesitate. In the same way the people of Nineveh must have blenched at the sight of the procession which Esarhaddon describes so complacently: 'I hung the heads of Sanduarri and of Abdimilkutte round the neck of their nobles . . . to demonstrate to the population the power of Ashur, my lord, and paraded (thus) through the wide main street of Nineveh with singers (playing on) . . . harps.'[2]

In a list of twelve kings of the coastal regions who

[1] The passage is as follows: Jehu wrote them [the nobles of Samaria] a second letter in which he said: 'If you are for me and if you will obey my orders, take the heads of your master's [Joram's] sons and send them to me tomorrow at this hour at Jezreel.' Now the royal princes, seventy in number, lived with the nobles of the city who brought them up. When they received the letter, they took the royal princes and slew all the seventy, and they put their heads in baskets and sent them to Jehu at Jezreel. A messenger came and said to him: 'They have brought the heads of the royal princes.' He answered: 'Put them in two piles at the entrance to the gate until tomorrow.' Comment is unnecessary.

[2] Text from Prism A in *ANET*, p. 291; extract in Dhorme, *RB* (1911), p. 204. Sanduarri was king of Cilicia, Abdimilkutte, as indicated above, reigned in Sidon.

had submitted to his power, Esarhaddon mentions, immediately after the king of Tyre, a certain Ba'lu, Manasseh (*Me-na-si-i*), king of Judah (*Ia-u-di*), and

XV. *Assyrian warriors counting severed heads (from Layard, op. cit., Pl. 26)*

after him the kings of Edom and of the Philistine cities, Gaza, Ashkelon and Ekron.[1]

Manasseh was in no position to offer any resistance and, to judge from the many marks of servility which he displayed, his overlord could not easily have

[1] Text from Prism B, in *ANET*, p. 291; Dhorme in *RB* (1911), pp. 210-11. Esarhaddon also deported populations, cf. Ezra 4.2.

found anything to complain of. Neither in the Book of Kings nor in any of the prophets is there mention of the sudden change of fate which, according to the author of Chronicles,[1] was meted out to the rebel king, that of being sent to Babylon. But this event is not incompatible with the information from Assyrian sources, for it is recorded that twenty-two kings of Hatti were summoned to Nineveh,[2] and Manasseh may have been among them.

The power of Assyria became more and more oppressive, and Esarhaddon succeeded where all his predecessors had failed: he entered Egypt and occupied Memphis (671 B.C.). King Tirhakah, apparently, was able to escape, but among the prisoners who, with a great mass of booty,[3] were taken to Assyria, were his wife, his sons and his daughters. The prophecy of Isaiah (20.3-6) was fulfilled to the letter and Egypt, that 'broken reed'[4] in its turn suffered the same fate as all its neighbours. Pharaoh, however, was not yet conquered and the king of Assyria had to embark on a further campaign, in the course of which a sudden illness caused his death.

*   *   *

[1] II Chron. 33.11: 'The commanders of the army of the king of Assyria mastered Manasseh with hooks, put him in irons and took him to Babylon.'

[2] Prism B in *ANET*, p. 291.

[3] The three Egyptian statues recovered at Nebi Yunus in 1954 (see above, p. 23), certainly formed part of this plunder.

[4] Isa. 36.6; II Kings 38.21.

At Nineveh there was no break in the succession; Ashurbanipal, one of the dead king's sons, ascended the throne while another, Shamash-shum-ukin, occupied the throne of Babylon. This division of authority, which was in accordance with the wishes of the late ruler, nevertheless bore within it the seeds of the dislocation and ultimate destruction of the Assyrian empire. Ashurbanipal himself was drawn into ambitious ventures and immediately began to plan a campaign against Egypt. Tirhakah, king 'of Egypt and Ethiopia'[1] had reconquered Memphis, 'forgetful of the might of Ashur, Ishtar and the other great gods'.[2] News of this reached Ashurbanipal in Nineveh. Having 'lifted his hands and prayed to Ashur and the Assyrian Ishtar', he mobilized his forces and travelled by the shortest route to Egypt. On his way to the Nile valley he raised contingents of troops from the twenty-two kings of the Phoenician coast-lands. Manasseh (*Mi-in-si-e*), king of Judah (*Ia-u-di*) was among those who brought gifts, kissed the feet of the king and provided soldiers.[3] Not only was Memphis promptly re-occupied, but the Assyrians, advancing to Upper Egypt, entered Thebes 'of the hundred gates' (663 B.C.). The fall of the

[1] This title is very carefully indicated in Isa. 20.3, in the words 'Egypt and Cush'.

[2] Text from the Rassam cylinder in *ANET*, p. 294.

[3] Text in the Rassam cylinder and Cylinder C, *ANET*, p. 294.

Egyptian capital caused a tremendous stir. The prophet Nahum utters this lament over it:

'Art thou of greater worth than No-Amon,[1] seated amidst
the arms of the Nile, surrounded by water.
She for whom the sea[2] was a bulwark and the waters a rampart?
Cush[3] was her strength and Egyptians innumerable.
Put[4] and the Libyans were her helpers.
And nevertheless she [is gone] into exile;
She has departed into captivity.
Even her little children have been crushed at the corners of the streets.
They cast lots for her nobles and all her great men were loaded with chains.'[5]

The biblical records which, as we have shown, carefully recount the sequence of most of the Assyrian kings from Tiglathpileser III to Esarhaddon, mention Ashurbanipal only incidentally and give a corrupt form of his name.[6] This king who reigned

[1] Nô-Amôn (= Thebes) is a form of the Egyptian Nut-Amen. The prophet here addresses Nineveh.

[2] The prophets sometimes call the Nile 'the sea' (cf. Isa. 19.5)

[3] Ethiopia.   [4] Somaliland.   [5] Nahum 3.8-10.

[6] In the letter sent by Rehum the governor and Shimshai the scribe to the Achaemenid king Artaxerxes '. . . the other nations which the great and noble *Osnappar* brought and settled in the cities of Samaria and in the rest of Transeuphrates' (Ezra. 4.10).

for more than forty years (668-631 B.C.) and whose realm now stretched from the Tigris to the Nile, no doubt had weightier preoccupations than the affairs of the tiny kingdom of Judah. He was always engaged in warfare on the borders of his territories: Elamites, Arabs, Manni, Cimmerians all had to be held at bay, away from more vulnerable areas, to say nothing of the Babylonians who were perpetually in a state of insurrection. At Jerusalem, Manesseh, who had been 'buried in the garden of his palace' (II Kings 21.18) had been succeeded by his son Amon (642-640), whose brief reign was ended by an army plot and assassination. The people, however, were loyal to the monarchy and to the reigning dynasty, and Josiah became king as a child of eight and occupied the throne for thirty-one years (640-609 B.C.). These dates are only approximate. The so-called Reform of Josiah, initiated in 622 by the prophet Jeremiah, could not have happened except for a concatenation of unhoped-for circumstances: Ashurbanipal had been dead for four years and his successors were showing themselves to be unequal to their task. The enslaved territories were able to shake off their chains and break their bonds. Their former masters no longer had the power to stop them, whatever they did.

It is hard to understand why the fall of Assyria was so complete and so rapid. Never had the empire been so great or seemed so mighty. And indeed it was mighty. For one hundred and twenty-five years it had been sustained by continuous endeavour which had never relaxed. For six generations the throne had passed from father to son[1] so that the kings, assured of that permanence on which the power of a dynasty depends, were able to survive all crises and to bring to completion a remarkable achievement. What they achieved was, it is true, the enslavement of the world, effected by means and methods so savage and brutal as to defy description—there is no reason why the facts should be concealed, for their authors made no secret of them; on the contrary, they boasted of them. All the decorations of their palaces are inspired by the same themes: hunting and warfare. Fighting lions (fig. XVI) provides the best training for the battlefield and, even allowing for their boastfulness, there is no doubt that the Assyrian kings often risked their own lives. The excellence of their generals did not relieve them from the obligation to take part themselves, and the kings of Nineveh did not fail to do so. They appreciated the more keenly, when they returned from their distant campaigns, the cool shade and beauty of their gardens, where, reclining on a couch, goblet in hand, they recounted to their queens the tale of their exploits. Musicians played soft music, fans swung gently, but in this idyllic setting there

[1] Sargon II, who succeeded his brother Shalmaneser, was the only exception, but it was still the same family.

was one dark spot: the bleeding trophy, recalling, even in that peaceful retreat, the savagery of war. Only a few paces away from Ashurbanipal, feasting in his arbour, may be seen hanging in a tree, the head of Teuman, victim of the last expedition against

XVI. A lion hunt. Assyrian painting from the palace of Til-Barsip (*from Thureau-Dangin*, Til-Barsip, *Pl. liii*)

Elam.[1] The whole character of Assyria is represented in these contrasts. War is never absent. Peace is of little account, being never more than an unstable armistice. The doors of Ishtar's shrine were never closed for long.

Nevertheless, in spite of its insecurity and lack of stability, the civilization of Assyria produced works of great beauty, not only in the material and economic spheres but in letters and the arts. Esarhaddon carefully supervised his son's education, and

[1] This is the well-known relief of Ashurbanipal 'in his arbour' now in the British Museum. Moortgat has recently suggested that it represents the myth of Tammuz, but this is open to grave objections.

[73]

Ashurbanipal, besides being skilled in riding, chariot driving and archery, had been taught 'the science of writing'. Thus it can be understood how his court came to be a home of the arts. Sennacherib

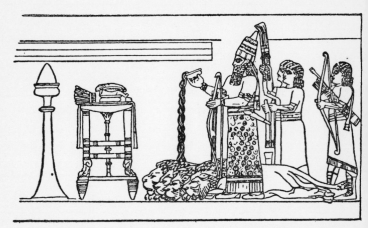

XVII. Ashurbanipal pouring a libation on lions killed in the hunt

had made Nineveh his capital, Ashurbanipal made it a city of artists and writers. The technique of carving bas-reliefs had never before reached such a high degree of development in Mesopotamia. The walls and apartments of the palaces were covered as far as the eye could see with tapestries of carved stone.[1] Not merely work on a grand scale, like that of the time of Sargon, but masterpieces: the reliefs

[1] The decoration of the palace of Khorsabad alone consists of about six thousand square yards of reliefs.

of Ashurbanipal's hunting (fig. XVII) are one of the high peaks of artistic achievement. In addition to sculptors, writers also were active. Not only did they record contemporary history on prisms, cylinders or slabs of gypsum, but they copied the literary works of the earliest times. In the royal library clay tablets preserved the epics and the mythology of a vanished world,[1] in which, however, these thorough-going realists found inspiration and instruction. Nineveh was indeed 'the great city'. But her end was near; for that colossus, like so many, had feet of clay.

[1] The most important groups of these are: seven tablets of the Creation, twelve tablets of the epic of Gilgamesh, the legends of Etana, Adapa, Zu, etc.

III

THE END OF NINEVEH

THE DEATH OF Ashurbanipal (631 B.C.) marked the last epoch of Assyrian history.[1] At Nineveh Ashur-etil-ilani succeeded to the throne and was followed four years later by Sin-shar-ish-kun[2]— both sons of Ashurbanipal. At Babylon the unknown[3] Nabopolassar had replaced the vassal of Assyria, Kandalanu, and founded an independent dynasty. The final act in the drama was quickly played out, and it is easy to understand how Zephaniah, who was living in Jerusalem at the time of Josiah (640-609 B.C.), could announce the city's impending ruin:

'And he shall stretch out his hand towards the North
     And destroy Ashur.

[1] New data on the last Assyrian kings, with revised dating, have been published in *Arch. für Orient. Forsch.*, XVI, 2 (1953), p. 310.

[2] Although elsewhere names have generally been written 'joined up', here they are given with the syllables separated, to assist the non-specialist reader.

[3] This is the meaning of the expression 'son of nobody' which is used here in the title.

[76]

He will make Nineveh a solitary place
    And a land dry as the desert.
Herds shall make their home there,
    And all the beasts of the fields.
The owl and the heron
    Will roost among her pillars;
The owl will cry at her windows
    And the crow on her thresholds.
See what has befallen the joyous city,
    Who queened it without a care
And said in her heart:
    "There is none like me!"
How has she become a desert
    A resort for the wild beasts!
Whosoever shall pass by her
    Will hiss and wave his hand.'

Zeph. 2.13-15.[1]

Thanks to a cuneiform tablet deciphered in 1923[2] the circumstances in which the city was captured and destroyed are now known. A Babylonian chronicle of events between the tenth and the seventeenth years of the reign of the king of Babylon

---

[1] Translation from the *Bible du Centenaire*.

[2] C. J. Gadd, *The Fall of Nineveh, The newly discovered Babylonian Chronicle*, No. 21, 901, in the British Museum; Dhorme, 'La fin de l'empire assyrien d'après un nouveau document', in *RB* (1924), pp. 218-34; J. Plessis, in *Livre du Cinquantenaire des Facultés Catholiques d'Angers*, 1925, pp. 197-209.

gives in fact both the date of the disaster (612 B.C.) and an account of the successive episodes as they happened. Nineveh fell under the attacks of an alliance formed by Babylonians, Medes and Scythians. Operations began in 616 B.C. with a Babylonian advance into the Middle Euphrates valley, an area which the Assyrians, fully aware of its strategic importance, had occupied for centuries. From the excavations at Mari much has been discovered about this campaign, so that it is now possible to gain a clearer understanding of how it must have ended.

However, the Egyptians went into action, forgetting that only quite recently the Assyrians had been their implacable enemies. By a reshuffling of alliances, of which history can show many examples, Egypt and Assyria were reconciled and Psammeticus, the Pharaoh of the time (663-609 B.C.) sent an army to the help of the hard-pressed Assyrians.[1] This intervention was not decisive, but the threat was probably averted for a time. In 615 the Babylonians met with a check before the walls of Ashur (Qalaat Sherqat) (fig. XVIII), but at this point the Median

[1] Dhorme, *loc. cit.*, p. 228, considers that this alliance 'might explain the famous prediction of Isa. 19.23, which has caused so much difficulty to exegetes: "In that day there shall be a road leading from Egypt into Assyria; Assyria shall come into Egypt and Egypt into Assyria and Egypt shall worship with Assyria." ' The original text, as most of the translations make clear, definitely does not say that Egypt and Assyria will worship Yahweh.

support reversed the balance of forces. The army of
Cyaxares, which had already appeared on the scene
at the end of 615, returned in 614. In the middle of
the summer they took Tarbisu, only 3½ miles from
Nineveh, but did not attempt to attack the capital,

XVIII. *Murals from Ashur (from W. Andrae,* Das
wiedererstandene Assur, *p. 29)*

which says much for the strength of its defences.
They turned aside to Ashur, which was taken with
fierce fighting.[1] Nabopolassar and Cyaxares decided
to join forces, but the season was now far advanced,
and the two kings retired to their respective capitals.
Obviously the days of lightning warfare had not yet
arrived!

In 613 the Babylonians made a fresh advance on

[1] The passage from Nahum 3.12 is exactly applicable to
Ashur and Tarbisu: 'All your fortresses are like fig-trees
laden with the earliest figs, which, at the first shaking, fall into
the mouth of him who would eat them.'

the Middle Euphrates, but the Assyrians met and repulsed their assault. The year 612, which was to be the last, arrived. The Babylonians and the Medes, who had now been joined by the Scythians, launched a large-scale attack. Fighting went on for several weeks. In August Nineveh was taken. The king and a number of officers were killed but the garrison was not wiped out and a detachment managed to escape. A new king, Ashuruballit, established himself at Harran, a city in the far west between the Tigris and the Euphrates. This was to be the penultimate royal residence of the Assyrians, and the seat of the last government. Two years later (610 B.C.) the Scythians and Babylonians swept away this shadow of power.

Ashuruballit again retreated and went to Carehemish in Syria. Again the Egyptians went to his help, but in vain. Assyria, fatally wounded, was in her death agony. Even while she reeled under the shock, however, she was able, indirectly, to deal a last blow at the kingdom of Judah which King Josiah had freed from its bondage—not only in the religious but also in the political sphere. When Pharaoh Necho (609-594) went to the aid of the Assyrians, the king of Judah prepared to intercept him and prevent the passage of his supporting forces.[1] He awaited them in the valley of Megiddo, the pass over the mountains of Carmel. Josiah

[1] On this point it is necessary to revise the earlier translation in view of our more accurate knowledge of the events. Instead

[80]

was killed on the battlefield in a chariot action, but his troops carried his body back to Jerusalem (II Kings 23.29-30). This national disaster cast a terrible shadow over the delirious joy with which the people had greeted the news of the fall of Nineveh. The words of Nahum may be quoted here:

1. 12. Thus saith Yahweh: 13. 'And now I will break the yoke which [the enemy] has laid upon you, and will tear your bonds apart.'

14. 'As for you,[1] this is what Yahweh has commanded: "Not one of your house shall keep your name alive.[2] Out of the temple of your gods I will cause carven images and statues of metal to disappear. I will pillage your tomb, for you are cursed."'

And now he gives the great news:

15. 'See upon the mountains runs the bringer of good tidings who proclaims peace!

of 'Necho marched *against* the king of Assyria', the passage should read '*towards* the king of Assyria', as in the *Bible du Centenaire*, and Father de Vaux, *Les Livres des Rois*, p. 220, note *a*. The text of the Book of Kings should be compared with the account in II Chron. 25.20-26, which is discussed, from the egyptologist's point of view by B. Couroyer in *RB* (1948), pp. 388-96.

[1] King Shin-shar-ishkun (see above, p. 76).

[2] It appears that the successor of Sin-shar-ish-kun (to be identified with the famous Sardanapalus) was not his son, but one of the higher officials (Gadd, *The Fall of Nineveh*, p. 19).

F   [81]

Keep your feasts, oh Judah; fulfill your vows,
For never again will you see the wicked one travers-
ing your land. He has been altogether destroyed.'

The prophet recalls for his hearers the last moments
of the beleaguered city:

2. 1. 'Climb upon the ramparts, to keep watch,
to keep guard.[1]

3. The shield of the valiant ones is red; the mighty
ones are clothed in scarlet. The drivers bring [their
chariots] into line, flashing with steel; the horsemen
brandish [their arms].

4. The chariots go raging in the streets, dashing
across the open spaces. Their appearance is like [flam-
ing] torches. They run from all sides like lightning.

5. At the signal, the warriors of the nobles rush to
their standards, they dash forward and cause [the
enemy] to stagger. They form columns and hurl themselves against the walls of the city, and the covering[2]
that shelters the assailants is set up (fig. XIX).

6. The gates of the water-courses are opened.
Terror reigns in the palace.

7. The queen is brought out; she goes into exile.

[1] In the Assyrian reliefs, the ramparts are always manned.
Here the roles are reversed: it is for the defenders of Nineveh
to repulse the assault.

[2] These are mobile defences used to protect the assailants
from arrows, stones or torches hurled from the ramparts, which
are frequently shown in the reliefs (see also fig. IX).

Her maidens also are carried away, moaning like doves and beating their breasts.

8. Nineveh is like a pool from which the water has drained away. "Halt! Halt!" But no one turns back.

9. Plunder the silver! Plunder the gold! There

XIX. Siege of a city (from Layard, op. cit., Pl. 43)

are stores of treasure without end, precious things of every kind.

10. Emptiness, desolation, waste![1] The heart fails, the knees tremble. Sharpness of sorrow pierces all loins. Every face is flushed. The city is doomed and helpless. She is surrounded, and all her efforts are in vain.

[1] The Babylonian Chronicle (line 45) reads: 'the spoils of the city, more than could be numbered, they took for themselves and they [reduced] the city to a mound and a ruin.'

3. 13. See, your men of war are like women in your midst. The gates of your land are wide open to your enemies; fire has consumed your barriers.

14. Draw water for a siege: repair your fortresses. Tread the clay, trample the earth, handle the brick-moulds.[1]

15. Nevertheless the fire will devour you, the sword shall destroy you.

3. 1. Woe to the blood-stained city, wholly given up to deceit, gorged with plundered wealth, given over to robbery!

2. Hark to the cracking of the whip! Hear the rumbling of the wheels! The horses gallop, the chariots leap.

3. The horseman mounts on his charger; the sword glitters, the lance flashes lightnings. There are wounded everywhere, the dead lie in masses! Bodies without end, they stumble over the corpses.'

It is the end, and now rejoicing and jubilation break forth:

'All who hear of your fate will hail your fall with joy. For on whom indeed has your cruelty not been poured out unceasingly?' (3.19). Cruelty: no word could more fittingly bring this *Te Deum* to a close.

*　　　*　　　*

[1] This is a remarkable touch of local colour; in that region, although there was abundance of stone, all the walls of cities were built of burnt, that is, sun-dried, brick.

One other voice is to be heard, however, that of Yahweh speaking to Jonah and sending him to Nineveh, 'the great city' (Jonah 1.2). At first, indeed, to proclaim its destruction exactly in the spirit of Zephaniah and Nahum. But the end is quite different: the city is to be spared because she repented at the prophet's preaching. As Adolphe Lods has written, this is clearly a 'parable', 'in its strangeness one of the most profound and the most evangelistic in the Old Testament'.[1]

The historical background gives rise to some difficulties. The statement that 'it was three days' journey to cross' the city (3.3) at once raises a problem, and some exegetes consider that this is an indication, among others, that the story was written long after the destruction of Nineveh, 'which was already wrapped in the mists of legend'.[2] But it may be suggested that the solution is to be sought elsewhere. Just as today, that part of London which lies within its ancient boundary is very different from what is called 'greater London'—a term which includes the suburbs and denotes a much larger area —so it may be that people who lived far away from Assyria understood by the word 'Nineveh' what is

[1] A. Lods, *Histoire de la littérature hébraïque et juive*, p. 593.

[2] *Bible du Centenaire*, note *b* to Jonah 3.3. Diodorus of Sicily (2.3) gives a more moderate estimate—seventeen miles in diameter, or one day's march. In fact at its widest, from the gate of Ashur to the gate of Nergal, the site measures approximately three miles.

now known as 'the Assyrian triangle' (fig. II), which stretches from Khorsabad in the north to Nimrud in the south, and, with an almost unbroken string of settlements, covers a distance of some twenty-six miles.

On the other hand, the mention of 'more than a hundred and twenty thousand people who cannot distinguish between their right hand and their left' (4.11) does not seem to be exaggerated. Felix Jones estimated that the population of Nineveh might have numbered 174,000 persons,[1] and quite recently, in his excavations at Nimrud, M. E. L. Mallowan discovered a stele of Ashurnazirpal on which it is recorded that he invited to a banquet the fabulous number of 69,574 guests. Mallowan considers that, allowing for foreigners, the population of Kalakh (Nimrud) might have been 65,000.[2] But Nineveh is twice the area of Nimrud, and thus it may be reckoned that the figure in Jonah 4.11 is indirectly confirmed.[3]

But the book of Jonah was a 'parable',[4] showing that in the eyes of Yahweh, the God of all the earth,

[1] Quoted by Campbell Thompson, *op. cit.*, p. 125.

[2] M. E. L. Mallowan, 'The Excavations at Nimrud (Kalhu)', 1951, in *Iraq*, XIV (1952), p. 21.

[3] D. J. Wiseman, 'A New Stela of Assur-nasir-pal II', in *Iraq*, XIV (1952), p. 28.

[4] The Abbé Feuillet (*Le livre de Jonas*, p. 15), regards it as a 'moral tale'.

even the guiltiest city—and Nineveh was red with
the blood of the peoples she had destroyed—could,
by repentance obtain the divine mercy and pity.[1]

XX. Assyrian bull from the palace at Khorsabad

[1] A. Lods, *op. cit.*, p. 584.

EPILOGUE

In 597 b.c. the prophet Ezekiel was deported to Babylon. By what road did the long column of prisoners make their way from Jerusalem to the scene of their exile in lower Mesopotamia? We do not know. Since they did not, apparently, cross the Syrian desert, two roads were open to them: one following the course of the Euphrates to Babylon; the other, a longer route, through Upper Syria, rejoining the Upper Tigris and leading down into the plain. Supposing the second alternative to have been adopted, the prophet would have seen the Assyrian palaces, demolished by the Babylonians and the Medes, but with their great winged bulls still standing guard, ineffectively and helplessly, over the royal gateways (fig. XX). If not, Ezekiel would have seen nothing of this imposing architecture, but it cannot be doubted that, when he arrived in Mesopotamia, he would have heard about it, for Babylon prided herself on being the heir of Nineveh.

It seems certain, in any case, that Nineveh was not to be forgotten, when, in his vision of the divine chariot, Ezekiel saw those strange beings, man, bull, eagle and lion in one (Ezek. 1.10), identical with the great stone guardian spirits of the Assyrian palaces—bulls with human heads, lions' breasts and eagles' wings. The man, the lion, the bull and the eagle are also elements in the Gospel symbolism. And so Nineveh, though laid in ruins, has left us this unexpected and, for the most part, unsuspected message. A mysterious heritage, bearing echoes and influences of the distant but undying past.

ASSYRIA	DAMASCUS	PHOENICIA
Tiglathpileser I (1114–1076)		Assyrians reach the Mediterranean coast
Ashurnazirpal II (883–859)		Phoenician cities pay tribute.
		Ithobaal (Tyre) (883–872)
Shalmaneser III (858–824)	Adadidri (Ben-Hadad)	
	Battle of Qarqar (854 B.C.) War against Israel Hazael	Phoenician cities pay tribute
		Tribute
Adadnirari III (810–782)		
Tiglathpileser III (745–727)	Resin	Sibittibi'li of Byblos Hiram of Tyre
Shalmaneser V (726–722)		
Sargon II (721–705)		

ISRAEL	JUDAH	EGYPT	REFERENCES
Judges Saul David (*c.* 1000 B.C.) Solomon The Schism		XX Dynasty	
roboam I 22–901)	Rehoboam (922–915)	XXII Dynasty (Sheshong)	I Kings 16.25
nri 876–869)			
ab 869–850) ELIJAH	Jehoshaphat (873–849)		
ttle of Qarqar aziah 850–849) oram			Annals
ram 849–842) hu 842–815) ibute to alamaneser II LISHA	Ahaziah (842) Athaliah (842–837)		
			Black Obelisk
ash 801–786) roboam II 786–746) HOSEA	AMOS		
achariah allum lenahem 745–738) ekahiah	Ahaz (735–715) Tribute paid to Assyrians		II Kings 16.7-8
ekah 737–732) oshea 732–724) ege of amaria (721)			II Kings 17.5
all of Samaria End of King- dom of Israel eportation of Israelites			II Kings 17.6, 24 18.9-11

ASSYRIA	BABYLONIA	JUDAH
Sargon II (721–705)	Merodach-Baladan (Marduk-apal-iddin) (722–711)	Hezekiah (716—687) ISAIAH MICAH
		Tribute paid Sargon
Sennacherib (704–681)		Campaign of 7 Capture of Lac
	Assassination of Sennacherib at Babylon	
Esarhaddon (680–649)		Manasseh (687–642) Tribute to Assyrians
Ashurbanipal (668–631)	Shamash-shum-ukin (668–648)	
	Kandalanu (647–626)	Amon (642–64 Josiah (640–60
Ashuretililani (630–627)	Nabopolassar (625–605)	JEREMIAH ZEPHANIAH NAHUM
Sinsharishkun (626–612)		
Fall of Nineveh (612)	Alliance of Babylon, Medes, and Scythians against Nineveh	
Ashuruballit (611–606) at Harran		Josiah killed at Megiddo (609

PHOENICIA	EGYPT	REFERENCES
	XXV Dynasty	II Kings 20.12–14 Isa. 20
	Shabataka (701–689)	II Kings 18–19 II Chron. 32 Isa. 36-37 Taylor's Prism Relief from Nineveh
ɔdimilkutte ᶦing of Sidon	Tiharkah (689–663)	II Chron. 33-11
ᵃ'lu King of ᶜyre	Assyrians enter Egypt	Stele of Sendjirli Isa. 20.3-6
	Assyrians capture Thebes (663) Psammeticus (663–609)	Nahum 3.8-10
	Nechao (609–594)	Zeph. 2.13-15 B. M. Tablet No. 21,901 Book of Nahum
	Egyptian-Assyrian Alliance	II Kings 23.29-30

SELECT BIBLIOGRAPHY

The bibliography includes only the most important works of reference, omitting the more technical or specialized monographs.

EXCAVATIONS

BOTTA, P. E. and FLANDIN, E., *Monument de Ninive découvert et décrit par M. P.-E. Botta, mesuré et dessiné par M. E. Flandin*, 5 vols. in folio, 1849-50.

LAYARD, A. H., *Nineveh and its Remains*, 2 vols., 1849.

—— *The Monuments of Nineveh from Drawings made on the Spot*, 2 vols., 1849-53.

—— *Discoveries in the Ruins of Nineveh and Babylon*, 1853.

SMITH, G., *Assyrian Discoveries*, 1875.

CAMPBELL THOMPSON, R. and HUTCHINSON, R. W., *A Century of Exploration at Nineveh*, 1929.

For details of the latest excavations at Nineveh, see the bibliography in my *Archéologie mésopotamienne*, I, pp. 437-8.

For the further exploration of Nimrud, see reports and studies by M. E. L. Mallowan in the archaeological journal *Iraq*, 1952 onwards.

For the continuation and conclusion of the excavations at Khorsabad, see Loud, G., *Khorsabad*, I, 1936; II, 1938.

A general account of one of the Assyrian capitals is given in Andrae, W., *Das wiedererstandene Assur*, 1938.

ASSYRIAN RELIEFS

BUDGE, E. A. W., *Assyrian Sculptures in the British Museum, Reign of Ashur-nasir-pal*, 1914.

PATERSON, A., *Assyrian Sculptures, Palace of Sinacherib*, 1915.

KING, L. W., *Bronze Reliefs from the Gates of Shalmaneser, King of Assyria*, 1915.

HALL, H. R., *La sculpture babylonienne et assyrienne au British Museum*, 1928.

GADD, C. J., *The Assyrian Sculptures, British Museum*, 1934.

—— *The Stones of Assyria*, 1936.

SMITH, S., *Assyrian Sculptures in the British Museum. From Shalmaneser III to Sennacherib*, 1938.

Bibliography

WEIDNER, E. F. 'Die Reliefs der assyrischen Könige', in *Arch. f. Orientalforsch.*, 1935-9.

Encyclopédie photographique de l'Art, Nos. 10 and 11, 1936. Reliefs in the Louvre.

HARE, S. and PORADA, E. *The Great King, King of Assyria*, 1945. Reliefs in the Metropolitan Museum.

ASSYRIAN TEXTS

LUCKENBILL, D. P., *Ancient Records of Assyria and Babylonia*, 1925-7.

Texts relating to the Old Testament have been published in two collections:

GRESSMANN, H., *Altorientalische Texte zum Alten Testament*, 1926.

PRITCHARD, J., *Ancient Near Eastern Texts relating to the Old Testament*, 1950, translations (pp. 265-301) by L. Oppenheim.

DHORME, *Les pays bibliques et l'Assyrie*, 1911, in which are collected studies published in the *Revue Biblique*, 1910-11. This is still the standard work.

—— 'La fin de l'empire assyrien d'après un nouveau document', *Revue Biblique* (1924), pp. 218-34. This article discusses the tablet in the British Museum, No. 21,901, published by Gadd, C. J., in *The Fall of Nineveh*, 1923.

For more detailed studies, reference may be made to the publications of R. F. Harper, *Assyrian and Babylonian Letters*; L. Waterman, *Royal Correspondence of the Assyrian Empire*, 1930-6; R. H. Pfeiffer, *State Papers of Assyria*, 1935.

For the time of Sargon particularly, see F. M. Th. de Liagre Böhl, 'Das Zeitalter der Sargoniden nach Briefen aus dem königlichen Archiv zu Nineveh', in *Opera Minora*, 1953, pp. 384-422.

ALT, A., *Kleine Schriften zur Geschichte des Volkes Israel*, II, 1953. A collection of studies concerned with the events which led to Assyrian intervention in the history of Palestine:
'Tiglathpilesers III erster Feldzug nach Palästina', pp. 150-62;

'Das System der assyrischen Provinzen auf dem Boden des Reiches Israel', pp. 188-205;
'Neue assyrische Nachrichten über Palästina', pp. 226-41;
'Die territorialgeschichtliche Bedeutung von Sanheribs Eingriff in Palästina', pp. 242-9.

ASSYRIAN MONUMENTS AND THE OLD TESTAMENT

The most characteristic are pointed out in the following works:

GRESSMANN, H., *Altorientalische Bilder zum Alten Testament*, 1927.

JEREMIAS, A., *Das Alte Testament im Lichte des Alten Orients*, fourth edition, 1930.

PRITCHARD, J. B., *The ancient Near East in Pictures relating to the Old Testament*, 1954.

In addition, valuable information is to be found in Grollenberg, Luc H., *Atlas van de Bijbel*, 1954.

CHRONOLOGY OF THE KINGS OF ISRAEL AND JUDAH

Very careful and detailed studies of Palestinian chronology have recently been made by a number of specialists: Thiele, Mowinckel, Albright and Alt. The following works are specially recommended:

THIELE, E. R., 'The Chronology of the Kings of Judah and Israel', in the *Journal of Near Eastern Studies*, III (1944), pp. 137-86.

—— *The Mysterious Numbers of the Hebrew Kings*, 1951.

—— 'A Comparison of the Chronological Data of Israel and Judah', in *Vetus Testamentum* (1954), pp. 185-95.

ALBRIGHT, W. F., 'The Chronology of the Divided Monarchy of Israel', in *BASOR*, 100 (1945), pp. 16-22.

—— 'The Date of Sennacherib's Second Campaign against Hezekiah', in *BASOR*, 130 (1953), pp. 8-11.

Critical Editions of the Bible (for the Book of Kings). A. Lods in *Bible du Centenaire*, 1947.

REV. FATHER DE VAUX, *Les Livres des Rois*, 1949.